We Deserve Better

A book to change the narrative for blacks
and other minorities

RODNEY CARRINGTON

13TH & JOAN

For permission requests, write to the publisher, addressed "Attention: Permissions Coordinator," 205 N. Michigan Avenue, Suite #810, Chicago, IL 60601. 13th & Joan books may be purchased for educational, business or sales promotional use. For information, please email the Sales Department at sales@13thandjoan.com.

Printed in the U. S. A.

First Printing, November 2023.

Library of Congress Cataloging-in-Publication Data has been applied for.

ISBN: 978-1-961863-23-1

DEDICATION

THIS BOOK MEANS so much to me for so many reasons. For one it is the first book that I have authored and it comes from my heart and my experiences which I wanted to pour out to the world to help young blacks and minorities that don't have the proper guidance around them. I would like to first and foremost give all thanks and glory to God for the anointing over my life. I feel like the things I have experienced are all to be a testimony to help others and I want to thank God for that. This book is first dedicated to my two sons Casey and Teagan. Being a dad changes you especially when you are blessed with boys. All I ever want for them is for them to be better than me, live life to the fullest, and live life the right way. I always said, "If I can teach my sons the wisdom that I have now in my thirties when they are in their teens or twenties, then I did my job." That quote is why this book was created. The idea started off for my sons but I started to think deeper about where I am from and how I would like to help more young blacks and minorities that might need the same messages and wisdom. Secondly, this book is dedicated to everyone that has helped me along my journey to become the man I am today. Everyone needs someone and I have been blessed to have good teachers, advisers, and other important people along the way that believed in me and gave me advice and opportunities. Without others believing in me and telling me how smart I am, or how gifted I am, I don't know if I would have used the potential and turned it into reality. So, I would like to thank anyone that ever believed in me and seen something in me that I didn't see in myself. And lastly, I dedicate this book to the audience I am trying to reach with this book. To all the young blacks and minorities out there that think they don't have anyone that believes in them or don't have a chance in this world, I would like to tell them that that is not true. I believe in you and the world is yours to take. No matter where you are from, no matter your circumstances, and no matter what people say around you, you deserve better. I pray blessings for all that have inspired this book and I want to let my children and all young blacks and minorities know that you deserve better!!

TABLE OF CONTENTS

PREFACE

I NEVER THOUGHT I would be in the military and I never thought I would be an author, but today I can say I have accomplished both. Life is strange that way. As kids we all envision and dream of how we would like our lives to go. Let's just use the old saying, "If I knew the things I know now back when I was younger..." I can complete that comment with a lot of different endings. But my life's journey is what led me to writing this book and has given me more content for other books I am working on. Throughout my life I always thought of myself as a leader and loved helping other people. I would always lend a helping hand and talk people's head off about making a difference and dreams that I wanted to turn into goals and then reality. I have always loved all people no matter their race, sex or ethnicity. I view a person not by the color of their skin, but by the way they treat people and the way they think. As I became an adult and had children I have taken pride in being a dad. Being a black man in America is the hardest job you can think of and having sons is a blessing and a fear. One of my sons is fully black while my other son is mixed. Everyone knows that society says if you are mixed with black or if your dad is black then you are considered black. So even though both of my sons have the hardest jobs of becoming black men in America, my mixed son has it even harder because he has to live in a world that some black people don't consider him black enough because he has a white mother and some white people don't respect his white half because in their eyes all they see is him being black. They are such a blessing to me and I want the best for them in every way, but that is also the scary aspect of being a parent, especially of two black boys. If they don't have the knowledge and guidance, and if they don't carry themselves the right way then this world will suck them up and spit them out. On top of me teaching them the things they need to know to become a man in the correct manner, my biggest goal is to make sure they are better than me at certain stages of life.

With the man I have become throughout my thirty-four years of living and with planting the seeds of success in my boys, this book was manifested. On top of that I also coach AAU basketball and have had the opportunity to instill different life lessons and skill sets into the lives of a lot of other young men. I have started to believe that God created my life and journey to help and be a blessing to the next generation of youth. I thought it was upon me to just be a great dad, but as more and more youth come into my life, I feel the responsibility to give them the knowledge and help to make them the best they can be. This is why this book was created and why it is so important to me. I am putting my all into this book and I mean everything I say in this book because I want the person or persons that read this to get something out of it that will make their life better or more successful. If I can help my boys and other youth to learn things, experience life at a high level, and be successful at an earlier age than I did, then I feel as if I did my job. I would like to first thank God for my life, my journey and my blessings that have led me to writing this book. I would like to thank my boys and all the youth that I have helped so far throughout my journey because it has been a big inspiration to spread the knowledge in this book. And I want to thank my dad because we have not always been close, but he has always helped me be the best man I could be. When I was young I didn't always like my dad's approach, but as I became a man it all clicked and he is a big reason why I am so motivated and driven today. He is also a big reason why I am so passionate about being a dad myself. I would like to send a special thanks to him because he is the one that told me I need to put all my knowledge and wisdom in a book to spread to the world. And lastly, but not least, I would like to thank my wife. She has supported me from day one and has shown me what having a real partner is truly about. I am blessed to have these people and this book would not have happened without their influence in my life. Blessed, grateful, and inspired!

INTRODUCTION

N O ONE EVER said life would be easy, especially being a black person or minority in the United States. There are challenges and adversity around every corner, but that doesn't have to be a bad thing. Does it make things tougher, YES, but nothing that is gained easily is worth it. America is very flawed, but it is still a great country and we have a lot of opportunities that other countries do not have. I was born in Norfolk, VA but moved to the metro Atlanta area when I was four years old. I grew up seeing the rough parts of Atlanta and seeing my people struggle with being a part of their environment. I've also seen a lot of people being complacent and thinking where they were at was all there was in life. I have seen a lot of my people succeed in Atlanta and also leaving Atlanta and being successful. At the age of eleven I was fortunate enough to be able to go to Barcelona, Spain with a program called People to People, which was for student athletes. You had to have good grades but also be good at your sport and someone referred me to that program. To this day I still do not know who referred me, but I am so appreciative that they did. My parents raised the money for the dues to go on the trip and I was on my way for the first time outside of Atlanta other than visiting Virginia to see family. I was very excited about this opportunity, but also very nervous. I was going all the way to Spain by myself; no parents and didn't even know my coaches or teammates. All other kids were traveling from other cities and states. We all met each other for the first time once we got to Barcelona. Long story short, it was a very exciting and successful trip. My team won the championship for our age group and I won MVP for the tournament. I was on a confidence high and no one could tell me anything at that time. After that trip I knew the world was bigger than just Atlanta and there were so many opportunities to achieve goals, to be successful and never be complacent. Fast forward a few years and I was in college at Georgia State University and my first son was born. Being just twenty years old I didn't know what to do, but I did know I had a child that will depend on me and I had to make a way. I left college my sophomore year and went to the military. Life was showing me head on that things don't always go your way and that plans may have to change. I was forced to man up before my peers had to, but my adversity has made me the man I am today. I never thought I would ever be in the military, but I did four years in the Army. You have to be a strong-minded individual to be in the military. If you are weak mentally when you come in, you will be stronger mentally when you get out. The military was not the route I wanted to go, but it was the route I needed to go at that time. I was able to provide for my son, I finished college while being a full-time soldier and achieved my associate's and bachelor's degree, and I was able to travel the world. Once I got out the military I was a different man and my mindset was different. I was always disciplined and driven, but once I got out of the military in 2014 I had a new vision for life. I went straight from being in the military to getting my master's degree. I wanted to achieve as much as I could and make a way not only for myself but for my son and future kids.

I truly believe there is no excuse why we can't achieve what we want out of life. This book is all about passing gems of information to all blacks and minorities that need it. I know firsthand that life is not easy when you are black or a minority, but I know firsthand as well, that life is full of opportunities and blacks and minorities can get the same blessings in this life as whites when it comes to having a successful life. Having a successful life is all about what you make it. That does not mean we will all be rich or famous, but it does mean we all can live comfortably and accomplish things that we were told were out of our reach for blacks and minorities. This book is filled with information that I have gained by experiences, reading and researching, and learn-ing from other people firsthand. The things that are shared in this book are just the basis to achieving better and suc-cess as a black person or minority in this country. There is so much to elaborate on off the topics in this book, but for me it is all about teaching these things to the next generation ear-lier. I grasped many of these gems later in my twenties and early thirties, but my goal is for the youth to start doing the things taught in this book in their teens and early twenties.

This book will start off talking about the most import-ant concept of all; and that is your mindset and how you think about everything you do. I really wanted to start the book off with the topic of our mindset because the way we think is the basis of how every action we make follows. It is something that I piggyback on throughout the entirety of the book. The way we think determines our moods, how we get through tough times, and if we succeed or fail. It is something that may be overlooked a lot of the time, but it is so important to how you sprout as a person. Your mental is just as important as your physical.

After focusing on your mindset and trying to either build that mindset or change that mindset, I will go into why education is so important. The reason I follow the chapter on mindset with education is because they go hand in hand. Gaining education is also a part of the mind developing and growing. Education is not just going to school and getting a piece of paper saying that you graduated or got a degree in a certain field. After the education chapter, I will dive into more topics that will build us mentally and help us succeed earlier in our lives. It will all come together to get the better that we all deserve.

CHAPTER 1:

MINDSET

T IS MUCH tougher for black men, black women, and other minorities (in that order) to achieve their goals, to get jobs, to get into college, and to live the American Dream than it is for white men and women. That is not hard to see and has been the way of life for thousands of years. But, as a black man (and minority) I believe a lot of the time our mindset is to always blame the "white man" for everything that is or isn't happening for us in our lives. We always complain, argue, or fight saying that the "white man" is the reason for this or that, but we continue to sell ourselves short by not getting educated, relying on the government for assistance and putting ourselves in systems that are built to tear us down and keep us from progressing. With this mindset and way of doing things we are making it easier for the "white man" to control a narrative that they already have an upper hand with. With me having boys it motivated me to not only change their mindset as a Black American while at a young age, but also want to help other black youth and other minority youth to change their mindset and to change the narrative as well.

We can't stop a racist person from not hiring us, from pulling us over and harassing us, or from turning down a different aisle because we are coming in their direction in a store because that is the mindset they have. We can change the mindset we have, stop blaming other races and focus on getting educated and getting an education, start businesses, learn a trade, invest, and support and help each other the way other races and cultures demonstrate. We must take control of the narrative and that starts with our mindset. I want this book to help the black and minority youth to start new generational mindsets, but this can also help older blacks and minorities as well. Just because you are not in your teens or twenties anymore doesn't mean it is too late for you or you don't have the right to improve your life. It all starts with our mindset.

I am very big on education and believe every youth should get a degree in something, but I also know that every child does not learn the same and some youth may not make the type of grades that traditional schooling says would get them into college. That shouldn't be an excuse and shouldn't stop us as parents, guardians, and role models from encouraging the next generation to change the narrative. I encourage (highly encourage) all young adults to get a college degree even if they are (so called) not good students. With the right guidance and encouragement, the kid that had a hard time in school can get a college degree in a field that would work for them or gain the confidence to use their brain and expand to a field that they never imagined working in. It has to be a mindset and you have to want to get that college degree, but if school isn't the way a person wants to go there is still no excuse to do things that will continuously put us behind the eight ball and allow the "white man" to control the narrative. Regardless if you get a college degree or not, anything you do, whether it is start a business, go to the military, or become a musician, you still have to be willing to study and learn your craft. That is why your mindset is so important. It is either you want more for yourself or you make excuses for yourself. Our minority youth are very gifted and intelligent, but don't always feel like they are. Sometimes they need someone to tell them this, instead of older minorities teaching them the wrong ways to go or talking down on them. They need the older minorities to encourage them, guide them, and if we are in a certain position, sometimes help them accomplish a goal. We need to give them a path to follow. But older minorities must stop focusing so much on the "white man" or saying they can't do certain things because of this reason or that reason and focus more on bettering ourselves and our youth. Like I said before, it is either you want better for yourself or you want to make excuses for yourself. Every minority youth isn't Lebron James or Cam Newton and won't be able to go pro in sports and every youth won't go the school route and have a degree, but they can go to the military, start a business, or learn a trade. All these things I am throwing out there start with a different mindset than the one most minority are accustomed to. The majority of our minority youth have the mindset of blaming everyone else but themselves. We blame where we grew up, or that our fathers weren't there, or that we won't get hired because we don't qualify. A lot of our minority youth also have a low self-esteem mindset because they don't think they deserve better than what they have or what is around them. Well, I am here to tell our minority youth that you DO DESERVE BETTER, and I will explain in this book different avenues to take that can get you the better that you deserve. This book is not going to stop racism. It is not going to change that the "white man" does control the narrative in this country. But it will help form a mindset of going to get what you deserve instead of giving the "white man" every reason to say we don't deserve it. It will inform you on different ways to build a positive life; a life that you probably didn't think you could have as a black person or minority. I want to help inform and share knowledge of things I had to learn later in life but want young blacks and minorities to gain earlier in life. This information can also help older blacks and minorities change their lives around from positions they are in now because it all starts with your mindset. Negative thoughts bring negative actions. Making excuses on why you can't do something and anger toward what this country was built off of doesn't make any situation better for us as a black community. There is nothing wrong with being angry at how our community is treated and has been treated from the beginning, but I want to spread information on how we can use that anger to better ourselves, our situations, and our future generations. Let's stop having kids and setting them up for failure by teaching them these negative mindsets and wrong adult habits. This information is not going to be taught to our black and minority children in schools, but these things can change the narratives for our culture. These things can increase the number of black owned businesses, increase the number of blacks graduating high school and college, decrease the number of blacks that are in debt and have bad credit, and increase the number of blacks that own a home. These things are important, and we need to make them a priority for us today to build the mindset for the generations of tomorrow.

Why is our mindset so important as blacks and minority? Because if you look at the mindset that was set for us during slavery and the mindset that the "white man" had during that time can translate to the mindset of today with the black community and the "white man". During slavery the mindset of blacks was to be controlled and to have no say in anything at all. The white's mindset was to control and run everything and to be the superior race. As time has passed that same mindset for both blacks and whites has continued. Times have changed a little where blacks have gained some rights and have started to speak up for our community, but the concept is still the same and blacks are still not viewed as other races are viewed in this country. When we are in debt, have bad credit or do not have an education we are being controlled by the system that has been put in place today. When we are under government assistance and do crimes that place us in jail, we are controlled by the system set in place. We give the "white man" control, and we really have no ground to stand on. When we commit crimes and get arrested for them, we give the "white man" the opportunity to charge us with whatever time they think we deserve, which is another way to control us. We must take it upon ourselves to change that slavery mindset. We must stop allowing them to control the narrative. We have rights and opportunities now, but we are still in a mindset that we don't deserve better. It will probably never be equal between whites and blacks and other minorities, but we do have freedoms and rights, as well as opportunities to make our ancestors proud for all they fought for. It all starts with our mindset and changing it from a mindset of slavery and being controlled with no way out to a mindset of being in control and building wealth, opportunities, and different avenues for ourselves and our future generations.

Your mind is so powerful and it is the control panel for your life. You can be strong physically, but if your mental is weak then you are weak. If you are believing negative things, then negative vibes will follow. For instance, just starting your day off by saying a prayer of gratitude for a new day and then telling yourself that this day will be a good day and believing that the day will be good will bring you the vibe of a good day. Not saying that things will not frustrate you throughout the day, but having a positive mindset will not allow those things to ruin your day or mood. We only have 24 hours each day to live and really there are only 12-16 hours that we are awake to be productive. With a positive mindset if things go wrong during your day you would focus on clear thinking and figuring out how to prevail, while with a negative mindset we dawn on the situation and think about everything that is going wrong and how it can get worse. One saying that comes to mind is, "A mind is a terrible thing to waste." But I also believe a person is a terrible thing to waste because of having the wrong mind-set. Your mindset is the backbone to everything you do and accomplish and for blacks and minorities, we will need to change our mindset one by one and then as a unit to make changes and get all we deserve. Because we deserve better.

CHAPTER 2:
EDUCATION

E DUCATION AND KNOWLEDGE are something that NO ONE can take away from you. Education and knowledge don't have to be just school education. Building knowledge in an area or field that you are interested in is also powerful and can't be taken away from you. School is only one avenue you can take to get an education, but it doesn't have to be traditional school. There are shorter programs that can be taken such as trade school, online classes, and even learning by being hands on. Going back to what I was saying in the previous chapter, it is all a mindset. As minorities we cannot be lazy or be on the same level as white men and women. We must take it upon ourselves and continue to learn and continue to grow with knowledge. A family member of mine with a degree and with a career, wanted to venture out into other fields and other ways of making money. With another family member he started a construction business and met an older black man in the construction field that has been doing it for a very long time. This man took my family member under his wing and started teaching him hands on and feeding him with knowledge. This is what I mean by getting educated and gaining knowledge without going to school. This is also what I meant in the mindset chapter when I encouraged older blacks and minorities to help the black and minority youth to achieve and accomplish things when we are in the position to do so. We don't always have to give them the answer, easier ways out, or finances, but we can guide them and give them the knowledge we didn't have when we were in their shoes. It is all about helping the next person and generation to succeed, to know they deserve better, and to build their mindset to do positive things.

A degree is just a piece of paper to some people and nowadays you need more than just a bachelor's to even get considered. You must get a master's degree and certificates to fight for and be competitive for positions now. I loved it and wanted as many degrees as I could get. But the part about getting a degree, even just a bachelor's, that a lot of minority youth don't understand is the part of networking while in school. This is another form of education and building knowledge to get the better that we deserve. Networking is one of the best forms of education, in my opinion, and is so important for so many reasons. It allows you to meet people for your benefit as well as the benefits of others. Through networking you get to pick people's brains, gather ideas, and build relationships that can influence your life or lives of others. Networking not only builds working relationships and opportunities, but can build personal friendships as well. For instance, while in college you can get close with a professor, join a fraternity or sorority, or get in an intern program. These networking opportunities build personal relationships that can lead to job opportunities or positions that can have you referred to job opportunities. Networking is an endless form of education where you learn from multiple people and gain the trust of others to give you these amazing opportunities. This is a great way for people that may not have typically got to know you for whatever reasons, get to know the man or woman you really are. This doesn't have to be just in a school setting. If you are working in a particular field and want to expand in that field you should take the opportunity to network with someone in a position that you would want to get to. Pick their brains, ask about opportunities that may be coming up, and just be a personable person that is willing to put the work in to get what they want. This same concept can work if you are interested in fields or opportunities outside of what you are already associated with. Do your research on the field or opportunity, talk to someone that is already holding that seat and ask them how you can get to that level. Go to different events or meetings and never be scared to communicate and ask questions. Networking is such a great way to learn, to meet people and to be presented with great opportunities.

School is not the only way to become educated, but one important thing to do is always educate yourself. Reading is something that we should always do, especially as blacks and minorities. We should not only read about things we like and for our own pleasures, which still builds our vocabulary, reading skills, and understanding ability, but we should also read to gain knowledge. We need to read about things that benefit us, such as managing money, starting your own business, and how to fix things. We have heard our whole life that reading is fundamental, and that statement is very true. Even with that being true how often do blacks and minorities read, better yet, how many blacks and minorities can't read? This goes back to the slave mindset that during that time whites literally stopped blacks from learning to read. Why was it so important to make sure we couldn't read? Reading and understanding what you are reading had to be valuable to put so much effort in making sure we didn't have that skill. Our ancestors had to sneak and learn to read on their own and many of them died to obtain that skill. Now that we have the right and ability to learn to read, why not use it to better ourselves and our understanding of different areas of life? In today's society we are so hooked on watching TV, playing video games, or doing other things that don't really help us to succeed that we get away from reading and learning things on our own. The same way we can watch our phones, computers and TVs for our entertainment, we can use the same devices to read a book, article in the newspaper or magazine to help enhance our knowledge. We don't have to have a physical book or newspaper anymore so there are no excuses not to enhance your learning or knowledge. Reading just for thirty minutes to an hour a day expands your knowledge and allows your brain to be used in a productive way. That same thirty minutes to an hour we usually use watching our favorite shows or on our phones not learning anything. Like I said, reading is fundamental, and this simple phrase has been put in our face our whole life. They are giving us the answer and we are not even taking it seriously. But reading is just the first part of the skill; understanding what you are reading may be more valuable than the actual reading skill. To be able to understand the verbiage in a contract, notes and text used to study for a big test or the adventure and mystery in your favorite novel is powerful and valuable.

Out of all forms of learning, I believe the most efficient way to learn is hands on learning. When you learn something hands on you are putting the knowledge to use at that time. You are able to make mistakes, remember the steps, and learn other ways to complete the task faster or more efficient. Therefore, knowing a trade could be more important than having a degree. If a person is not good with school or doesn't want to go the route of college, then learning a trade could be a great route to go. With knowing a trade, a person will always have a job and this person is essential. Also, as a person perfects their trade, they can start their own business pertaining to this trade. Learning a trade by being hands on, which makes this person essential, and also learning to run a business for your trade are all forms of education and gaining knowledge. This could all be done without going to traditional school, but could make you and your family wealthy, as well as help teach and provide knowledge to the next generation.

The biggest thing we need to work on as a culture is to stop being lazy and making excuses. There is no excuse and no reason to not educate yourself in some form or fashion. We all learn differently, but the key is that we ALL LEARN!! You are going to have to get educated or be educated in some form or fashion no matter what you do in life. School is not the only form of education and to be honest everything in school is not correct. There are so many ways to learn and gain knowledge and if you want to grow in life and in your career, you will have to be willing to become more educated.

There are so many ways to gain an education and knowledge, we just have to make it a priority and have a mindset of knowledge is power. No one can take your education or knowledge away from you, but you can use that education and knowledge to be successful and to help others be successful as well. Things continue to change with or without us, so why not continue to learn and be a part of the change. We deserve better and being educated is a part of that reality.

CHAPTER 3:
GOOD CREDIT

HAVING GOOD CREDIT is something that I didn't take seriously until I needed good credit and is something that is not taught in the majority of black homes or to black youth. Of course, they do not teach this very important subject in schools, so I want to give insight on how important it is to have good credit, how easy it is to mess up your credit, and how hard it is to fix your credit when it is messed up.

Let's start with how easy it is to mess up your credit. Since you are not taught in school the importance of good credit, that means it is easier for blacks and minorities to mess up their credit. It is easy to get credit cards and stir up a lot of debt because that is what the system is set up to do; put you in a lot of debt and make it hard to pay the debt and interest off. If you do this at a young age, it will stop you or make it hard for you to buy a car that you want, purchase a home, and even stop you from getting certain jobs. Once again stopping us as blacks and minorities from getting the better things that we deserve. A lot of blacks get things on credit and have the mindset that they have the merchandise and not worried about paying the debt off or they get credit cards and spend up the limit and either pay the minimum or don't pay it back at all. Maxing out a credit card or going over a certain percentage of your credit limit will affect your credit in a negative way. Not making consistent payments or paying at all affects your credit in a very negative way as well. Paying the minimum on time each month can help your credit, but it is a slow-moving growth when credit cards are maxed out or the amount of credit is high. When having a credit card, experts say the usage rate should stay under 30 percent and be paid consistently on time to get the best credit score. A lot of the time the mindset is that we will pay it off later, but if we allow it to go to collections that makes your credit go down as well. The more things that are negative on your credit (not paid on time) or the higher your credit card usage is, the lower your score will go and that will hinder you from not only getting a lot of important things but stop you from using credit in the future. Another thing that can mess up your credit is getting personal loans. Personal loans can be very helpful if you have a plan on paying them back and can help build your credit if you pay them back on time, but they can be very hard to pay back without a plan because they come with a lot of interest on top of the principle amount that is owed. If you get behind or don't pay them back, personal loans can be very harmful to your credit. As I mentioned, it is easy to mess up your credit. Credit can be easy to get. The system wants you to use credit, but you have to have the mindset to use it responsibly and not put yourself in situations where you have a whole bunch of debt.

Now let's talk about how hard it is to fix credit once it is messed up. My credit is good now, but it took way longer to fix it than I would like. It was so easy to mess up, but the process to fix it is long and fixing your credit doesn't happen the way you would think it should happen. Let's say you are in your thirties and decide that you want to fix your credit to buy a house, get a new car, or just begin to think differently than you were thinking in your twenties and want to fix a few early mishaps, including your credit. You would think all you would have to do is pay off all things that are in collections on your credit report and that would make your credit score shoot sky high, right? Wrong!! Fixing your credit doesn't work like that and shows another system of controlling minorities by making it so easy to get credit, use credit, and mess up your credit, but when trying to fix it, the process is slow and long. I am not telling you to not pay off the things you have in collections on your credit because that should be the first thing you do, but I am saying paying those things off will not automatically make your bad credit score shoot up to a very good credit score. There are four key steps to fixing your credit score:

- Paying off all items in collection
- Disputing any items that you don't think are supposed to be on there or that have incorrect information
- Get new credit, like a small credit card to build up consistent payment history
- Keep your credit usage 30 percent or lower

Starting with the first step of paying off all items in collection; this is very important and needs to be done first. You may not be able to get any new credit if creditors see these unpaid accounts on your credit. You should prioritize the accounts in collection from smallest amount due to largest amounts due and pay them off in that order. Once you prioritize them, call the collection agencies and see if they will settle for an amount that is less than the amount that you owe. Some collection agencies will settle for a lower amount, and some will not, but it is good to ask. Once the amount is agreed on, ask them to set up payment arrangements if you cannot pay it in full at that time. It is best to focus on paying one off at a time, but this is where the process of getting your credit fixed starts and appears longer than the process of messing it up in the first place. When I was cleaning my credit up, I was so excited to have a plan and start to knock off one collection at a time. I thought once I paid all the collection accounts off my credit score would shoot to 750!! I was very wrong and highly disappointed. Paying off collection accounts will only boost your credit score up a few points when it is first paid off. It is not something that automatically makes your credit score increase. But this is still a to-do because over time your credit score will rise because these delinquent accounts are paid off and you will be able to get new credit that you will strive to pay on time. After paying collection items, you should focus on credit card limits that are high or anything that is behind on payments that has not reached collections just yet. Late payments and high limits on credit cards will be the next negative after collection items that are really harming your credit. Once collection items are paid off and other highly used accounts are getting paid on time and paid down, then you will start to see your credit score go up and you will be able to use your credit more often.

The next step would be to dispute anything that you believe is not supposed to be on your credit report. It does not hurt your credit score at all to dispute items and can help your score a lot to get things taken off. There are two ways to win a dispute of an item on your credit report:

- If the information that the collection agent has for this account is incorrect in any way you would need to dispute to get the information corrected, such as wrong amount due, wrong addresses, or account already paid in full.
- If the collection company doesn't respond back on the account in the amount of time given to respond. (30 days)

We will start with the easier of the two, which will be the collection company not responding back. The dispute, once it is filed, is held for 30 days. This is the process where the credit bureau reaches out to the collection agency to get all information supporting that this is your account, and all information is correct and up to date. If the collection agency doesn't respond for whatever reason within the 30 days, then this account will be taken off your credit report. This is not a quick process, so you must stay on top of the process when the dispute is filed, but it is worth it to do.

The other way to win a dispute or to get corrections on your credit report is when the dispute is filed and if it is confirmed that the information on the account is not correct. This is when the account holders do respond to the credit bureau when a dispute is filed. When an error is found, make sure to dispute this mistake with each major credit bureau, send documents to prove that this is incorrect and keep records of anything you send in. Just like any dispute process the credit bureau has 30 days to investigate. If the credit bureau looks at your request as being "irrelevant" they will stop their investigation. They will have to notify you with their reasoning, or they may ask you for additional evidence to prove your request. All information you send to the credit bureau is also sent to the business that reported that information. The business will investigate as well and send their findings back to the credit bureau. If they find that they are incorrect, they must notify all major credit bureaus with the correct information, and this will help your credit score improve. The credit bureau will also have to send the corrections to anyone who got your report in the past six months, if you ask them to do so. They would also have to send it to anyone who got a copy for employment in the past two years if you ask them to do so. These are things that are not taught to young blacks and minorities, but these little nuggets of information and knowledge can change your life and help you from being stuck in a system that wants to keep you ignorant.

Having good credit is very important, but it is even more important to know what to use credit for and how to allow credit to work for you. I learned later in life that I wanted to use cash more than credit. I had gotten myself in a lot of debt in my early years because I had the mindset of, I can pay this credit off later. Once I started to gain some financial maturity and understanding how important it is to be as debt free as possible, I worked hard to clean up my credit and wouldn't buy things unless I could afford it and had the cash to pay it in full. But I also learned that you could use credit to help you and not for credit to always be a burden to you. I believe each person should have at least two credit cards. You should have a high limit credit card with a limit like $5,000-$10,000 etc., and a low limit credit card. The reason to have a high limit credit card is for going out of town on trips and for big emergencies such as major car problems, medical expenses, etc. I didn't have this knowledge in my early twenties. I learned it was a good idea to have a high limit credit card when I went on a big trip to Vegas with a group of friends. We got to the hotel and was attempting to check in and the hotel explained to me that they take debt and credit cards but to use a debt card they would put a bigger hold on the card than the actual expense of the room. I was young at the time and didn't have extra money just to be held for a room; I needed my money and calculated every dime to have fun on the trip. One of my closest friends had a high limit credit card at the time and explained to me that I need to eventually get one for things like big trips and major emergencies. High limit credit cards can really help build your credit and have a lot of different perks to come with them like cash back and different promotions. In my opinion, I think you should only have one high limit credit card because it can be so easy and tempting to spend them and buy things that are not needed or necessary with the limit being so big. You must be very disciplined and aware of your spending, and even more responsible with paying your bill off and on time.

While having a high limit credit card is important, having a low limit credit card is just as important. These credit cards should be used in small emergency situations, such as between pay periods you need gas for your car, to get a tire for your car, or small grocery pick up to get through the week. Just like high limit credit cards, with lower limit credit cards you need to be responsible and pay the bill on time and not use the credit card for unnecessary reasons. Both high and low limit credit cards can be beneficial as long as they are used responsibly and paid on time. I believe having two credit cards is a good number because it allows you to build your credit while not overwhelming yourself with debt. I am not a fan of having a lot of different credit cards from multiple different stores. Every store offers their own credit cards now and I believe it is just another way to trap you into more and more debt which will ultimately hurt your credit and take all your money because you will be paying a lot of different unnecessary credit card bills. My wife is an example of being responsible when using and paying down your credit limit. While I believe two credit cards are enough, my wife doesn't have a problem with having more than two or three credit cards as long as you have a strict plan with paying cards down and keeping the usage right low. Once again, I prefer to stay away from a lot of unnecessary credit and use cash to pay for most things, but most importantly be responsible and take care your credit.

Some other things to stay away from that are easy to get but can really mess up your credit, are personal and payday loans. The only type of loans that you should get are car loans and home loans. Any type of pay day loan or personal loan is a trap and can put you more in debt than you were before you attempted to get the loan. Payday loans and personal loans are so easy to get but can be so hard to pay back. Have you ever heard the saying, "Anything easy to get is not worth it"? If you haven't heard that before, I am glad I can be the first to tell you that and that saying applies to everything in life. Easy money is not worth it because it can come with negative consequences such as troubles coming from where the money comes from, not appreciating the money and losing it all, or there could always be strings attached to easy or quick money. That is the case with anything given to you quickly or easily. When you work for something or earn it there is always a better sense of accomplishment and appreciation.

When it comes to payday loans and personal loans, they are easy to get but hard to pay off unless you know you will have the money to pay them off right away. If you don't have the money to pay that loan off quickly or make minimum payments, they usually are attached with big interest rates on top of the amount that you owe. With having to pay these ridiculous amounts of interest and principal you are losing more cash out of your pocket which is keeping you in the same situation you were in before you got the loan or making your situation worse than before you got the loan. On top of that, if you don't pay the loan back or miss payments it will affect your credit in a negative way. It is a big whirlwind of trouble from taking more money out of your pocket to affecting your credit in a negative way all for easy quick money that you will spend fast and probably forget what you spent the money on.

Lastly, having good credit can help you if you are trying to become a business owner. Having good credit shows banks and lenders that you are responsible, and they can trust you to pay your business loan payments on time and work toward paying the loan off. That is not to say people with ok credit or bad credit can't take the same responsibilities, but it is all about perception and the system is set up against us as blacks and minorities, so we must play the game to our advantage.

Credit is very important and if you have good credit, you can purchase anything, and it can also help you get certain jobs. I am a firm believer of using cash for almost everything, but I am also a firm believer of building your credit responsibly so you can get the home that you want and deserve as well as the car you want and deserve. You can start the business that you want as well, and you will not be trapped in a system that is set up to make sure blacks and minorities don't get what they deserve. This is coming from a man that experienced taking the hard route by messing up my credit and having to build it back up. I have seen the advantages of having good credit and what it can help you accomplish, and also seen what bad credit can prevent you from achieving and setting you back.

Credit can become good or bad depending on how you use or abuse it. These things are not taught to blacks and minorities in school and most of the time it is not taught in our homes, but it is important to be informed about how to use credit in ways that are responsible and that will help you not only in the short term, but in the long term as well. Credit is a subject to become educated on, as well as having a mindset of using it the proper way to help you succeed in life. Credit is just another system used to prevent us from getting things we deserve, but when we are informed and using it the proper way we can use it to our advantage. The same advantages that anyone or any culture uses it for when taught the importance of credit and benefits of good credit.

CHAPTER 4:

HAVING A SAVINGS ACCOUNT

ONE THING THAT I was not good at when I was younger or disciplined enough to do was start and keep a savings account. This is something that a lot of our young minority do not do, they do not know to do, or know the importance of doing. Majority of our minority people (young and older) live paycheck to paycheck, while putting ourselves in more debt along the way. This is a recipe for disaster!! It is a cycle that never gets broken because A. no one teaches us otherwise and B. it is so easy to accumulate debt. We have already learned a little about debt and ways to stay out of debt in chapter three, but now we will focus on the importance of saving and how easy it is to do without it really hurting your finances.

It is so important to save your money starting at a young age because you don't have as many responsibilities and can be more flexible with your money and also train yourself to have money put away for a rainy day. You may need a new tire, you may lose your job, or you may want to put a down payment on a house or car. There are so many reasons to have a savings that you build consistently. Minorities get so consumed with spending that we make everyone else rich, and we have nothing to show for it. Every time you get paid or get a lump sum of money you should have a designated amount that you put away in a savings account first before you do anything else with the money. Ideally, I would say put 10 % away, but the way you save may be different than the next person. The most important thing is that you save, not the amount you save. First to remember when saving is to be DISCIPLINED. Don't always put money away, but then dig in your savings just because it is there and take little chunks out of your savings. We must remember that savings are a part of your portfolio (which we will talk about in the next chapter), for emergencies, and to break the cycle of living paycheck to paycheck. Savings are a backup plan. If you don't think you can be disciplined with a savings account that you can have access to regularly, then get one that has regulations on how much money you can take out or when you can take money out. Once again, the most important thing is to be disciplined with your savings, know the amount you are able to save, and focus on the purpose of your saving.

There are so many ways to save your money and it is best to start young or as soon as possible. If you are older, it is not too late to make saving a habit and to know how important it is to have a savings account. Blacks and minorities should set goals for themselves on how much they would like to save per pay period, how much they want to save monthly, or even how much they want to save annually. I know a lot of youth are not thinking about saving for the future, but they should think about saving to get things they want like a new pair of shoes, a car for when they go to college, or money to go on a spring break trip with friends.

This stops us from living paycheck to paycheck, adding debt we do not need, or spending money on things we shouldn't at a certain time. As older minorities, we should be teaching our younger minorities the importance of saving so as they continue to mature, they will be saving for a future, for a new home, and to establish their own wealth. By us older minorities teaching this to the younger generations we are changing bad habits, generational curses, and the mindset of majority of our black people and other minorities. But us older minorities can't do these things and teach the younger generation if we don't know these things to begin with, so that is why it is important to share and spread the information in this book.

A lot of minorities don't make savings a priority because they may look at it like they need their money now. There are so many ways to save without the money that you are saving putting a hole in the money that you have and so call need. You can do the 52-week challenge for instance, that is very simple and after 52 weeks you have saved $1,378.00 in your savings. How the 52-week savings plan works is you basically save the number of dollars of the number week you are on and so on. For example, week 1 you save 1 dollar, week 2 you save 2 dollars, all the way until you get to week 52 and you save 52 dollars. This should be a whole year and at the end you should have roughly $1,378.00 saved. That is one of the simplest savings plans there is.

A lot of young minorities ask when the best time is to start saving. I always like to tell the youth to start saving when they get their first part time job. Young people can really start saving the first time they get an allowance. The earlier the better because it trains the mind to appreciate the money you make and not spend every dime you have. But let's say a young person starts when they get their first part time job. If a young person saves 50 dollars every time they get paid, they will build a nice nest egg to have for when they go to college, want to purchase their first car, or even in a broader scale they could use those funds to start a business that they envisioned on starting. 50 dollars a check for a young minority is a good starting point, but nothing wrong with saving more. Another good time to put money in a savings account is when you receive a big lump sum of money, such as student loan checks or tax returns. We must get out of the mindset of looking ahead at our big lump sums of money and spending it before we even have it. Black youth typically have the mindset to get tax returns or student loan checks and blowing it on material things or things that have no value and will be forgotten about not too long after purchasing them and then that money is long gone. Don't get me wrong, it is okay to treat yourself when getting larger amounts of money, but it will go a long way to take some of that money and put it in a savings account. One of the best ways to start a savings account is starting it with a large amount and building off that amount with a certain percentage each pay period after that. If you received a student loan check, for instance, that was $1,500 and put $1000 of it in a savings account and then every time you got paid bi-weekly from your part time job you save $100 it would grow at a rapid pace, and you wouldn't miss the money that was building in that savings. With that $500 left over from the student loan check and your left-over paycheck from work you could pay bills or treat yourself. That is how you spoil yourself and take care of yourself at the same time. When we receive money, either in lump sums or from our paychecks, we are going to spend the money anyway, so why not give yourself some insurance and stability by saving some of it. You must pay taxes and bills every time you get paid so why not pay yourself first and put some money away. Like I mentioned earlier, saving helps train the mind to appreciate the money you have and also taking care of yourself for the long haul. Spending money is taking care of yourself for the short term, while saving money takes care of you for the long term.

Another example to build your savings is taking the amount of money that was in your account before your next paycheck hit and put that amount in your savings every pay period. For instance, if I had $100 already in my account and then I got paid that day, I will put the $100 in my savings because now my check starts my pay period over. I wouldn't need that $100 and would probably waste it on something I don't need so it is a great idea to just put it in my savings. Every time I get paid, I would put whatever I had left over in my savings no matter if it was $10 or $150. An even more efficient way to save money is to have it taken out of your check to go directly to a savings account. That is probably the most disciplined way to build your savings. An allotted amount that you desire can be taken from your paycheck to go directly to your savings while the remaining amount goes to your checking account. You don't have to worry about transferring money to a savings account or changing the amount you save each pay period. You can consider this to be the same concept as when taxes are taken out of your check, except this money is coming to you and helping you for the long term.

The small examples that I have given on ways to save are typically used if you are using a traditional savings account that is attached to your checking account, but there are so many ways to have a savings other than the traditional savings account. A few other types of savings accounts are high-yield savings accounts, money market accounts, certificates of deposits, cash management accounts and specialty savings accounts. They are all used for different reasons, but as you mature and become more financially literate, different types of savings accounts could be helpful and build your portfolio. Traditional savings accounts are for short-term use and are used for emergencies and are attached to a checking account. They are usually flexible when it comes to taking funds out and usually allow up to six withdrawals a month. High-yield savings accounts are usually offered with online banks and they are saving accounts that offer a higher APY (Annual Percentage Yield) compared to a traditional savings. Annual Percentage Yield is the rate you can earn on an account over a year and it includes compound interest. I truly consider high-yield savings accounts, especially when you just want your savings to grow and hardly touch it for anything. Money market accounts are good forms of savings accounts to look into as well. They have combined features of a traditional savings with the features of a checking account. These are usually accounts at credit unions and online banks. One con to these types of accounts is that there may be monthly charges for these kinds of accounts. This next form of savings account I am a real fan of because with a certificate of deposit, or also known as a CD, you will always have money. CDs are time deposits, which means you agree to leave a certain amount of money in the account for a set period of time. During the time that your money is in the CD, you will earn interest and when the set time has ended or matured you have the option of taking the money out or rolling it over to a new CD. Cash management accounts are the next set of accounts but this type of savings account is not specifically designed for saving. These accounts let you hold cash that you may plan to invest in a taxable brokage account or in your retirement account. Finally, you have specialty savings accounts. Specialty savings accounts could be savings for minors, such as kid's savings accounts, custodial savings accounts or student savings accounts. They could also be education savings accounts, such as 529 college savings accounts and Coverdell savings accounts. Another example would be retirement savings accounts such as Traditional and Roth Individual Retirement Accounts and IRA CDs. And lastly, you have healthcare specialty accounts such as Flexible Spending Accounts (FSA) for childcare and Health Savings Accounts (HSA) for healthcare spending. There are many types of savings accounts and many ways to save. You just have to be informed on each type and see which best fits your needs. You may get to a point where you have a few savings accounts for different reasons. It is all about being financially literate and building your portfolio.

With all the tips and efficient ways to save, you cannot save efficiently if you have a lot of debt. Once I started working and making pretty good money, the first thing I told myself was there is no point in saving when I owe other people. What I meant by other people was debt and loans. There is no point of saving if you owe debts to a lot of different collection agencies. Not to say don't save if you have debts because a debt can be a credit card bill or a car payment, but if you are late on a bill, or personal loan payments, etc. then you should prioritize paying debt before saving a certain amount of money or lower the amount that you put away to save while you pay off certain debts. It is all about learning financial literacy, breaking generational habits and curses and knowing the system so we can be successful as blacks and minorities in this country. The goal is to have the least amount of debt as possible, and to build your portfolio and wealth not only for yourself, but your generations to come after you.

CHAPTER 5:
INVESTING

MY DAD ALWAYS told me, as well as hearing this quote from millionaires and billionaires, that to build wealth you must have more than two or three sources of income. You have your primary job, which is your everyday source of income, whether it is getting paid bi-weekly, weekly, etc. Even if that primary job is a very good source of income and you are living comfortably or better than just comfortably, it is not enough. The reason I say it is not enough is because with the ideas and knowledge that I am spreading throughout this book I am trying to build a mindset and wealth for not only you, but for your kids and grandkids as well. I am trying to establish a mindset that blacks and minorities can change their narratives and change giving all the power to the "white man". So, just having a primary job and source of income, even if it is a good source of income, is not enough. You must have other sources of income to build your wealth and portfolio. A great source of income is investing. Investing is a source of income that takes time, you must be patient with it, and you could lose money, but it is a source that builds for not only you, but your family, kids and so on. Two key forms of investing that I focus on in my own life are investing in companies and investing in real estate.

Investing in companies can be a great source of income and make you a lot of money, but it is something you must be patient with, and you must put money in to make money, hint to what the word invest means. This is something that when doing you have to be informed on and allow to build. I want to use this chapter to give basic information on company investing and basic terms that need to be understood. To expand your wealth and investments you should have an investment portfolio. The investment portfolio is separated by four asset classes: Equities, Fixed incomes, Derivatives, and Cash. In each asset class there are different securities. Let's break down each asset class and their securities.

Starting with Equities, they have securities such as stocks, mutual funds and ETF: Exchange-traded funds. Stocks are the easiest and most common of the three securities in the Equity asset class. Stocks are shares in ownership in a company. This means you own a piece of this company. The more shares you buy, the more money you can make if that stock is doing good. But you can also lose money when your stock is doing bad, and you can sell those stocks and use that money to buy a different stock that may be doing better. Once again, this is not a get rich scheme. Building wealth with stocks may take years and remember you must put a fair share of money in to make it beneficial for you to make money. When I started buying stock, I had a separate bank account than my primary bank account just to save money to buy shares of stock for different companies. It is difficult sometime to figure out what companies to buy stock in. I was always told to start by buying stock in companies that you know about, buy products from, or are interested in. It is also good to do research on up-and-coming companies that you can buy their stock for cheap at that time, and as they grow you will make more money off them as their stock prices rise. And lastly, you should look to buy stock in companies right after their IPO. IPO means initial public offering, which is when a company goes from private to public and shares can be purchased in that company. This is also known as a stock market launch. Stocks are a very good start to investing, but there are more options. Mutual funds are like stocks but differ in that they are investments that pull your money together with other investors to buy shares of many different stocks, bonds, and other securities that might be more of a challenge to do on your own. When you have one stock you have one share in one company, whereas if you have one mutual fund you have one share in many companies. Mutual funds are also a long-term investment that you must be patient with and allow to grow and mature over years. ETF, which means, exchange-traded funds are similar in how they operate to a mutual fund, but they are traded on the day-to-day stock exchange like stocks. ETFs can contain many types of investments. ETFs are a marketable security with an associated price that allows it to be easily bought and sold.

The second asset class is Fixed Income. This asset class consists of securities like Bonds, Treasury, and CDs (Certificate of deposit). This asset class's name tells you a lot about the investment and how they basically work. The name Fixed Income means the payments are essentially fixed or consistent in regular intervals. Bonds are issued by government and corporations when they are trying to raise money. When you invest in a bond you are giving the issuer a loan and they agree to pay you back the face value of the loan on a specific date. They also pay you interest payments along the way, usually twice a year. Bonds can have two potential benefits when they are part of your portfolio. They give you a source of income and they can offset any loss you may see from owning stocks. Treasury bonds are government securities that have a 30-year term. They earn interest until they are mature. The owner of the Treasury is also paid the principle, when the Treasury bond matures. A CD, or Certificate of deposit, which we talked about in the savings chapter, is a secure form of time deposit, where money must stay in the bank for a certain amount of time to earn a promised return. A CD almost always earns more interest than a regular savings account. I really like CDs because they build up for the time allotted, but like I mentioned before these types of investments take time to make money and you must be patient. This type of discipline changes the mindset of get rich quick and having money for the short term. This is building long term wealth and different forms of income.

The third asset class is called Derivatives. This class has the securities such as options, futures, and currencies. Derivatives are a financial security with a value that is reliant upon an underlying asset or group of assets. The derivative itself is a contract between two or more parties, and the derivative derives its price from fluctuations in the underlying asset. The most common underlying assets for derivatives are stocks, bonds, currencies, interest rates, commodities and market indexes.

The last asset class is cash. This consists of savings and money market accounts. I won't go too far into detail on savings because we just learned all about the importance and value of saving in the chapter before, but it can be added to your portfolio. Money market accounts and savings are very similar, but money market accounts pay higher interest rates than typical saving accounts if you maintain the minimum balance. This asset class doesn't grow as fast as the other asset classes, but they are good to have just in case you need money on a rainy day, and they are easy to access. These four asset classes put together create your investment portfolio and help build and organize your wealth. This helps you have more than one income and stop having the mindset of living paycheck to paycheck. This helps you build for the future and stop thinking in just the now. There is so much more information on these investments and when trying these investments you should build off the information I have given and get more in detail about them and their processes.

The second form of investment consists of real estate investments. I was told to have more than one income, but I was also told to have income that grows while you are sleeping, and this is that type of income. As you can see, every chapter in this book has a connection and the information goes hand and hand to change your mindset and build up your life, wealth, and opportunities. When I explain real estate investment, I am not telling you to become a real estate agent and sell houses, unless you want to go into that field of work. I want to explain how real estate for an average person can become a source of income that is not your primary source of income, but a source of income that builds even while you are sleeping. Like other methods in this book, it takes you investing your money to make more money, and it also takes having good credit to accomplish this investing. There are two ways you can go about doing this real estate investing, but they both deal with having good credit and starting by using your own money. The first method could take some time but can be the cheaper route of the two. Let's say you bought a house. To get a house you need pretty good credit and to have a nice amount of money saved. It is a process that needs to be planned out. This first house you purchase may not be the house that you want for the long term, but it is your first house, and it is a nice starter home. Buying a home is different than buying a car because buying a home is an investment and it increases in value. It can make you money. So, with this house that you have bought, every upgrade you make to the house makes the value of the home go up. You have bought new blinds for every room, you have planted different plants and flowers around the house, you have also built a fence around the house. Every upgrade added brings the value up on the home. It will seem like you have spent a lot of money adding things to the home, but it will be well worth it in the short and long road ahead. A few years have passed, you have good credit, a nice savings account and your career is going well. You have made a nice number of upgrades to your home and want to sell it and get something bigger and more of what you always wanted. Your first house is not paid off, but the plan is using that house as your "money while you are asleep" home. Buy the new house that you want and rent out the first home. With all the upgrades to the home and with the value up in the home you can rent the home out for more than what your mortgage price is. For instance, if your mortgage each month is $700, you can rent it out for $1200 and use that rent that is being paid to you to pay the mortgage and pocket $500. BOOM now you are making money while you are asleep and this is an extra income for you. To be smart about it, you should always put away 3 months of mortgage when renting out your home for emergencies, like if the renters up and leave without paying or break something, for example. When receiving the payments from the renters you should also not pocket the extra money at first. You should put that money in an account just in case something with the house needs to be tended to, because the house is still your home and your responsibility.

The second way to go about real estate investing is a quicker way of making money, but it takes you having a little money to use. This is buying homes or buildings and renting them out to people. Doing this type of real estate investing is for people that either have money, this book is not intended for them, or people that use different saving technics from the saving chapter. If you start saving and are consistent with it, you will be able to have a nice amount of money saved and can take advantage of opportunities like this. If you have the amount to buy a small home or building, you can invest in that home or building and upgrade it and go about it the same way I explained when renting out your home. The difference in this type of real estate investing is you can use the money made off renting out this home or building and purchase more properties and make money off more than one property. This is expanding the income sources you have and allowing you to make money while you work your primary job and make money while you sleep. We must expand our mind and opportunities. We must stop having a one-track mind and stop blaming the "white man" for everything that determines our future. While there are a lot of unfair advantages that other communities have, we also have different avenues we can take to not only better ourselves and our lives, but to think bigger and set up a future for our kids and loved ones.

There is so much to learn about when planning to invest and I only provided information on investments that I know about and have been interested in. These are small starter points and ideas. When trying to get into investing please do your research because you can lose a lot of money investing in the wrong things or listening to the wrong advice. Investing is a good way to build your financial portfolio when done correctly. I am a firm believer of continuous learning and investing is definitely a subject to really learn about if you want to take advantage of its perks.

CHAPTER 6:
STOP HATING ON EACH OTHER

A MINDSET THAT BLACK America must change ASAP is black people hating on black people. We also must stop black people killing black people but let's start with just the hating of black on black. This mindset of hating or going against your own race is what we see in the black community, while other races support each other even in times that they shouldn't. We can't expect the "white man" or anyone to respect us if we hate and hurt our own people. No one will take our fight for respect, justice, or equality seriously if we keep hating on each other, not supporting each other, disrespecting each other, and killing each other.

Before we go into deeper issues, we must start with what builds up to the deeper issues: blacks hating on other blacks and blacks not supporting other blacks. Black people seem to always hate on each other when one of us are doing good or better than another, accomplishing goals that we have set, or trying to make a better life for ourselves. We always call that person a sellout or talk down on them just because they are doing something different than we are doing. Don't get me wrong, there are some black men and women that have went on to better themselves and turned their backs on the black and minority communities, but everyone that goes into the corporate environment, politics, or outside the black community is not a sellout. We need minorities to spread to these other environments to get our voices heard. Instead of hating on them or talking down on them, blacks and minorities should support them and keep them accountable for the things they are supposed to be doing to help the blacks and minorities. We are lacking blacks and minorities in a lot of major roles such as CEOs, politicians, general managers, etc. Even more, we are lacking the support from the black community when a fellow black or minority has a major role. We should support and encourage our fellow blacks and minorities when they tell us their dreams and aspirations. You never know how that little bit of encouragement, or a few positive words can jump start this person into accomplishing the goals they have for themselves. No job or career is set for one race and while some jobs and careers are dominated by certain races, that shouldn't stop us from making history or exploring change. We get upset or always have something to say when our managers are white, our president is white, or white men have positions of power, but then we criticize blacks that are in these positions or working toward these positions by saying they are lame or sellouts. We need to stop hating on our own kind and build up our own kind. How do we expect others to take us seriously, if we don't believe in our own people?

Another big thing that is disappointing are black people not supporting black businesses. Humans have no problem spending money on things they want and need, so why do black people have a problem with supporting another black person's business? For example, if a shirt at Macy's or in the mall is $60, black men and women have no problem paying for it if they like it. We can go even bigger than that if we talk about the money Black America spend on designer clothing, shoes, purses, luggage, etc. People, black people especially, spend money on what they want to spend money on. But, if a black person is selling their clothing line and say the price of the shirt is $45, we tell them that is expensive or ask for a discount. Another disappointing example is an example given to me by a friend of mine, which is also my old barber. He explained to me in a frustrated tone that he was getting a lot of complaints from black customers when he raised his prices from $30 to $40 per haircut. In the same instance those same customers will go and buy the new Jordan's for $200 with no questions asked. What makes it even worse, he explained to me that he has white customers that always complain to him that he is lessening his value for his service. They usually pay him a lot more than he charges with no problem. I am not saying that all customers need to tip $50 when the cost is $30, but it is very frustrating to see customers complain about the cost of his services when he is actually cheaper than a lot of other barbers. Other clients even try to get over on him and pay him less than the price he charges. We must stop trying to get over on each other, and undermining each other. There are a lot of blacks and minorities that are building their brand and building their businesses and I strongly believe blacks should support blacks. Not only is it a way to support and encourage our own people and culture, but it is also the start to helping black own businesses and brands to compete with the other major businesses and brands. This is another example of how we must change our mindset. Other cultures and communities don't treat each other like this and help to build each other up. We need to do the same.

While blacks hating on each other is one concern, a bigger concern that branches off the hate is blacks killing one another. We always get upset and make a huge deal when a white person or white cop kills a black person, which is well deserved and makes total sense, but we need to make just as much fuss when we have senseless black on black killings as well. Most of the time when these killings occur it is for little to no reason at all. We kill each other over shoes or other material things, over someone calling us this or that name, or because we think we must look big and bad to everyone around us. When these pointless killings take place there are two lives being taken with one bad decision. The person that is actually being killed and the person who did the killing. You have a black person that is physically gone, life cut short and a family losing a piece of them, and you have another black person in jail for life losing all freedoms, opportunities, and two families living hurt because of their decision. We will not get the respect from other races and cultures when saying "Black Lives Matter" if we as blacks don't respect our race and culture first.

This chapter was not meant to be long and drawn out, but it is meant to really be put on front street that as a people we are our own worst enemy first and foremost. We have so many other obstacles in the world that are against us and want to prevent us from succeeding. We cannot be against ourselves and our own people as well. If we continue, that is like having a candle being burnt on both ends. We have to start supporting other blacks when they are doing well for themselves. We have to start supporting black businesses. When I speak on supporting blacks when they are doing well for themselves does not mean just giving them a pat on the back, but to keep them accountable for their positions and support their growth in helping other blacks and our community. When I speak on supporting black businesses, I don't mean just buy their product, but to give them a fair assessment. Give them a fair shot but let them know genuinely if the product is a good product. Spread the word about the business and product if it is a good product. Don't make a fuss about the price because if it is a good product then the price is well deserved, but if the product is not good or not what you would want, don't down the business. Just proceed with another business. It is a difference between constructive criticism and down talking something, but we have to know the difference and get away from downing each other. And the last thing that needs to happen is if you are a black person with power, position, or money you have to start genuinely helping your community. You have to give back to where you are from or where you see your community hurting. You cannot disconnect and separate yourself from your community because we need blacks in those positions to have a chance for change in our communities and in this world.

The bottom line is blacks need to stop hating on each other and stop killing one another. We have to support each other, encourage one another, help each other, and most importantly love each other. We will never gain respect or anything else due to us if we stay divided. Other cultures, races and groups of people are there for each other and that is why in a lot of areas they are surpassing us as a people. But we can take the steps to change this and stop burning on both ends of the candle. So, as a black man I want to say to my black community, "I support you, I am here to help you, and I love you."

CHAPTER 7:

MORE THAN AN ATHLETE OR A RAPPER

W E MUST NOT only change our mindset from always blaming the "white man" and not taking our lives in our own hands, but we also need to broaden our minds to be more than just athletes and rappers. There is nothing wrong with dreams of becoming an athlete or rapper and there is nothing wrong with working hard to become either one, but we must have back up plans or expand to other roles in those fields. We can work in those fields but have other roles that are behind the scenes, like sports agents or producers. As a culture we have taken over athletics and being a music artist, but there are plenty of areas outside those two that are lacking our culture, which means they are lacking our control. We do all the work with our talents, but someone, most likely that is white, benefits more from our talents. There are so many roles in fields that we are interested in that are lacking blacks and minorities; we just must start focusing on them. This chapter of insight also connects to the chapter on being educated. For a lot of these careers you will need to have a college degree, but in some instances, you just need to educate yourself on the craft at hand and establish some networking.

A lot of our black and minority youth think all rappers come from the hood and sell drugs. While a lot of them do come from that background, a lot of the artists we know, and love, also have degrees and other business ventures as well. The ones that have degrees and other ventures are good examples of blacks and minorities that use music as a starting point for their success. The rappers that are really from the hood or from a life of struggle are good examples of people not allowing their circumstances to define them. All the information that I am sharing connects to one another and proves that blacks and minorities deserve better and can become better no matter your circumstances. I am saying that because even being from the hood or from circumstances that put you behind the eight ball should not stop you from being successful or making a better way for you and your family. A lot of the rappers we love have used their position to get themselves out of the circumstances they were in before they were famous. They also used being an artist to venture into other business aspirations. This is very common for athletes as well. They have gone to finish their college degrees, start clothing lines, start their own record labels, invested in different alcoholic beverages, and so much more. This is a great example that shows education is important and having more than one income is important as well. This is also a great example of using your time and opportunities wisely and making the best out of the life you have. 2 Chainz is a great example of a black man that is more than just his music and more than where he started. 2 Chainz is from College Park, Georgia and was in the streets at a young age. Even with being in the streets 2 Chainz was a basketball player in high school, but what a lot of people don't know is he graduated second in his class. He also received a scholarship and played basketball at Alabama State University. Not only is he a well-known successful rapper, but he ventured in other businesses and as of 2019 he has acquired a minority ownership in the Atlanta Hawks NBA G League affiliated College Park Skyhawks. This is just one example of a black man that is magnified in the rap game but also is educated and has built himself in other business ventures as well. Black people are very talented in every aspect of life and can be more than just a rapper or an athlete. But we must know that about ourselves and have that mindset. We cannot expect others to believe in us as a culture if we don't believe in ourselves or each other as a culture. It all starts with our mindset. As young blacks and minorities we must use all our skills that God has given us as a people. Focus on becoming an athlete, but also have the degree in whatever field you are interested in just in case you don't go pro. Then use that platform to help the next minority youth to be better than you were. Be a minority agent and sign players and help them learn to manage their money correctly. Get a degree in sports medicine so you can help support that college team and its players. Work hard to become a singer or rapper, but also learn the music business so you can open your own recording studio or so you can understand the contracts that you are signing. Learn to produce your own music and network with other young minorities that are doing the same things that you are doing. A big example of being more than an athlete, that I admire very much, is

Lebron James. Yes, he is a super star basketball player, and he did make it big in sports, but not only is he venturing in other businesses, he has made a way and a lane for his closes friends to build businesses and opportunities, and he has opened up a school for less fortunate children to get a good education and to have a chance to succeed. In 2022, Lebron has officially became a billionaire. This is such an amazing accomplishment especially for a kid out of Akron, Ohio, as Lebron would say. Lebron came from a single parent home and in society every odd was against him. Since high school he had so much pressure on his back as the Chosen One, but it has never wavered him. We have never heard of Lebron cheating on his wife, getting in trouble with the law, or cheating the game of basketball. The only thing people argue and criticize is if he is the best to ever play the game of basketball. For all the people that don't think he is the best to ever do it, that is a conversation for another day, but if that is all that people have to say about him in a negative light, he is in very good shape, no pun intended. Lebron has done things the right way for himself, his family, and all the people around him. He has accomplished many business ventures such as investing in the Blaze pizza franchise, starting his video production company, and starting the web platform UNINTERRUPTED, just to name a few. His story is the ultimate example of being more than an athlete. Those examples of 2 Chainz and Lebron show that once you make it to a certain stature you should use that platform to help others, and venture into other realms to build your portfolio. To do things that people said you couldn't accomplish or that people like you had no business doing. Those two examples were to show that nothing is impossible, and that blacks and minorities not only deserve the same opportunities but are just as talented and smart as anyone else. I know the names that I mentioned have been successful and made it big in music as well as sports, but it is more important to know there are so many more things to do in those fields if you do not make it to being a rapper/singer or to the NBA/NFL/MLB. You can be around the sport you love or in the field you love and leave a major impact without being a player or musician. And to be honest those other positions need more blacks and minorities.

I do see a lot of positives coming from the next generation when it comes to being creative. There are a lot of youth in our community that understand that we are more than an athlete and more than a rapper. The internet and social platforms have played a big role in this new wave of creativity. The youth these days have been using social media to make money and have really taken advantage of it. From doing funny skits, to making new dances, it has really taken off to show more talents that our culture has. A lot of the youth today have decided that they don't want to do things in a traditional route. The school route was good for me. I loved school and learning and achieving degrees. But it seems this route is becoming more and more known as the old school route. That is not a bad thing if the newer routes are productive and allowing the youth to make a way for themselves as far as educating themselves and making a productive living. I encourage anything that allows our young blacks and minorities to stay off the streets, out of trouble and out of jail.

What I would love to see more than anything is our next generation and beyond to start imprinting their stamp in areas that typically do not have a lot of blacks and minorities. It is well known that blacks and minorities run the majority of sports (no pun intended) and have taken over the entertainment business, but we are more than rappers and athletes. I would love to see more young blacks and minorities becoming dentists, doctors, politicians, and more. In a lot of these uncommon fields like being a politician it is hard because we have to push out these old white men to really get a chance, but we have to have the ambition to even try to make a path for ourselves. If we have mindsets that we can't do it or we don't belong then things will never change and that is what the traditional older white people in those seats want in our society. We have to stop looking at certain fields as boring or look at them as if we don't belong. We definitely need more blacks in professions like doctors and teachers. On a small scale, it is so encouraging as a black man to go to the dentist, doctor's office, lawyer's office or to a school and see a young black man or woman in those positions. Nothing wrong with other races or older blacks in those positions, but when there is a young black man or woman in those positions, as a black man I feel more comfortable and they are relatable. It is a feeling that I will be taken care of when in their hands and that they actually care about me and my situations. Even more, we need more black men in these fields. For example, we need more black men in the school systems to help lead these young men and women. Women have done a very good job with teaching and leading kids the right way, but especially for young black male youth, it would be so aspiring to have more male figures help them with school, internships, tutoring programs, and developing into men from boys. The black and minority youth need someone they can relate to. They need someone that has been where they have been and have gone through things they are currently going through. Most importantly, they need someone that has done well for themselves to show them that no matter where you come from or what your circumstances are, you can still become something in life and you deserve more out of life. That is very important because being a black man is the hardest job in the world. Black men are looked at as a threat, which is far from the truth. To turn that narrative around we need black men to show our youth by leading by example instead of allowing the world to tell our youth these lies. We need more black men in leadership roles and to influence our youth by mentoring them and showing them there are multiple paths to take to be successful.

Young blacks need to know and understand that they are more than athletes and more than rappers. It will always be a blessing to have the talents to become an athlete or musician, but I want to help build the mindset for our youth to use those platforms in music and sports to not only take care of yourself and your family, but to also venture into other businesses. Use those platforms to give back to your community and make a way for others to achieve their goals. You can be whatever you want to be. You are not limited to being an athlete or musician; you can be a doctor, lawyer, painter, dancer, and so much more. Young blacks and minorities are so smart and talented and are needed in so many areas and fields in this country and in this world. Sometimes you just need someone that sees things in you that you may not see in yourself and I want to start by being that encouraging push for you. Young blacks and minorities: YOU ARE VALUABLE!!

CHAPTER 8:
TIME

TIME IS THE most important, but most overlooked and underappreciated aspect of human life. As young people we think time is on our side. We think and say things like, "I can do it tomorrow ", or "When I get older I can...". In reality your time is now, and your focus must be on doing what's best for you and focusing on your goals now. The older you get the faster it seems like time is passing and life is blowing by. You hear a lot of older people saying they wish they did this or that when they were younger, or they wish they could have changed this or that. With that being said, I am advising the younger generation to understand that time waits on no one. And, you don't know how much time you have on Earth, so use your time in a productive way.

Using your time in a productive way can also be rephrased as using your time wisely. I heard the phrase use your time wisely over and over as I grew up, but it didn't click to me until I was in my late twenties. Starting at a young age you should use your time wisely in everything you do. If you are an athlete and your goal is to be the best athlete you can be and make it in your sport at a high level, (whatever the level should be) you must use your time wisely. Most athletes have practice between two to five times a week with their team. That is standard, but what do you do when you are not with your coaches and team? How are you using your time? Are you on your phone looking at social media, are you watching a lot of TV or playing video games? Or are you getting better at your craft and sport? If you want to get better at whatever your craft is you must work on it when no one is watching or when no one tells you to do so. You must work on your craft when you don't want to work on your craft. That is using your time wisely. Not to say that you can't use down time to chill, watch a little TV, or use that time to do whatever you want to do, but you don't want to make it a habit of wasting time that could be used to be productive.

Using your time wisely doesn't have to be just for an activity. This can pertain to your everyday life. Work on training your mind to make everyday a productive day. Use your time to learn something new, to read a few chapters of a book, or to work on a craft that is important to you. Make everyday count because life is too short and every day that passes that you don't do something productive is a wasted opportunity and pushes you further from your goals. There are 24 hours in a day. You sleep 6-8 hours of that day, which leaves you with 16-18 hours left to be productive. Most people are in school or working 8 hours a day, which leaves you with 8-10 hours left in your day. One of those hours you use to get ready in the morning, and three of those hours are used to eat breakfast, lunch and dinner. Out of 24 hours on a typical day you have 4-6 hours of free time. How do you use that free time each day? Time goes by so fast, and everyone is always on the go so I know a lot of people want to use those 6 hours or less to sit down and relax for a minute or two. Nothing is wrong with relaxing after a long day, but don't let it become a habit of wasting the few hours of free time that you have daily. If you are an athlete go put up a couple of shots, go to the batting cage, or go swim a few laps. If you are writing a book, take some time to jot down some ideas. Or if you have a few goals you would like to work toward and accomplish (short term and long term) take an hour and map out your plans and think about next steps to achieving those goals. The same amount of time we use to watch a show, look at social media or play video games, we could be using to be productive for ourselves. Like I have mentioned before I am not saying having chill time, watching tv or being on social media is a bad thing, but I am saying break some habits of using your free time everyday doing things that are not productive to your life.

The big reality with time is that you do not know how much time you have on Earth. I know when we are young, we think we will live forever, and we have so much time to do certain things or to change and grow and improve. But that is far from the truth. The truth is only God knows how much time we have on this Earth, so we need to appreciate the time we do have and make the best of it. Older blacks and minorities need to instill this in the minds of the younger generations. We must teach our youth the importance of knowing you only have one life so live it to the fullest but protect your life at the same time. What do

I mean by protect your life? Protecting your life is trying to make the best decisions for you and keeping yourself away from things that can harm you or your life's trajectory. Make the best of the one life you have and never let a person or situation dictate the way your life will go. It is hard to tell a person that is going through a hard time or that has an unfortunate way of living to make the best of the one life they have, but you cannot let your circumstance make you. YOU MAKE THE CIRCUMSTANCE!! You allow your life to be a testimony for the next person. Use the time that God gives you on this Earth to become the first person in your family to get a college degree, to work toward your goals, to make your kid's lives better than what you experienced growing up, to buy a house, and to travel the world and enjoy life. There will always be obstacles and things that try to prevent you from obtaining better, but if you allow these situations to dictate your path of life, time will continue to pass, and your opportunities will be wasted. If you have time, why not use it to do positive things for yourself and for others. Let every second count, pun intended.

Everyone gets the same amount of time each day, but everyone uses their time differently and the way you use your time could be the difference between being successful and being unsuccessful. Being successful doesn't always have to do with monetary gain. Being successful could be you putting in the effort and using your time to help others, or to create something, or even just to learn and gain knowledge on something. When time is wasted it seems like the candle of life is burning faster. Like I mentioned, we don't know how much time we have on Earth so we have to really think about how we want to be remembered. How did we use our time to affect others and leave an impact on this Earth? Time doesn't just affect you, but it affects your loved ones as well. Appreciate your family and good people around you. Send people a text consistently and give people a call to check up on them because life is short and we need to spend more time loving one another and being happy. We have to start using the time that we have thinking in a more positive manner than holding grudges and being negative, especially when it comes to people close to us. So many times we have thoughts like, "I wish we would have talked more." Most times, things that we are upset about are not that serious or could be fixed and we need to appreciate each other more than we have in the past. We need to show more love and appreciation for each other and our time together.

Lastly, everything is about timing and things have a prime window. What I mean by that is I don't like when people say you have time to complete this or that. Some things need to be planned out and take time but everything has a prime window. The easiest example is the life span of an athlete. An athlete must make the best of the years that they are in peak form and shape. If they don't then their potential and talent is wasted because they didn't make the best of their time. This could be the same with someone selling homes because the market is better in certain times. The market fluctuates so if you don't use that peak time, you could miss opportunities. You have to take advantage of prime times. This is important in almost everything in life. Never use the excuse that you have time or you can do this later. Life is short, life is precious, and we have to use our prime years and prime opportunities to maximize our life.

Time moves at a steady pace, but if it is wasted it will seem like time flies right by. You will go from the age of 16 to the age of 40 real fast and feel like you missed out on so many opportunities and missed out on so much time that you could have spent with people you love, on trips enjoying life or just being the person you wanted to be. Time is precious and we need to appreciate every second God gives us on Earth. So I would like to conclude by saying stop thinking you have more time than you really do and live life like every day is your last, and use it to achieve something, learn something, help someone, and love more.

CHAPTER 9:

STAY ON THE STRAIGHT AND NARROW

ONE OF THE biggest forms of slavery and controlling mentalities today is the locking up of African Americans. Once a person is convicted as a felon and has a record, this country we live in has made it so your life can be just about over. How it is set up, there is no serving your time for your crime and getting your life back on track. Once you have served that time for the particular crime, your life has just become even more difficult. You will get out of jail with a record. As a felon, it is very difficult to get a lot of jobs. Without a job you cannot provide for yourself or your family. So that leads to you doing things that you did in the past or something else illegal to provide and putting you right back in jail. As a felon, you cannot vote. You lose a right that our ancestors died for us to be able to do. Without your vote we lose voters that can help put the person we need in positions that could help our community and country as a whole. As a felon, you cannot own a firearm. Not to use a firearm in a negative way, but you cannot have a firearm to protect your family from negative situations in this world. You can't even own the firearm to go hunting for game or to feed your family. As a felon, you cannot travel out of the country. You can't experience other cultures and go on trips with family and friends unless they are in the US. You are trapped in this country with bare minimum rights. The land of the free where you are no longer free.

The main key is we must be on top of our game as blacks and minorities at all times. We cannot get relaxed and feel like certain things can't happen to us. One bad decision can destroy our lives forever. We don't have a concept called "Black Privileged". We don't get three strikes: not even two strikes. We have one opportunity to make the best of our lives and we should also use that to make the lives better for the black youth after us.

We must stay on the straight and narrow. I tell my sons to always watch who you hang with and watch your environment. This is something that all young African Americans should live by. When I say watch who you hang with or around, that concept could be a general concept. This could be a concept to be careful of all people. But, when I tell my boys this concept, I am particularly speaking about their white peers. I don't care what color your friends are, but I want my sons to understand, and all young blacks to understand, you cannot do the same things that white people do and think you will get the same results. For example, there are three friends, two are white and one is black, and they get in trouble by the police for loitering in front of a store. The two white kids get rude and disrespectful with the officer. Please understand as an African American we cannot act in that matter. No one should act like that in these situations, but we don't have the same leeway as African Americans that white people have. As African Americans we must watch what we say, how we say things, and watch what we do. It is unfair, but we must be on our P's and Qs at all times. I focus on teaching my sons the little things that seem to be forgotten in this world. I teach them to say please and thank you, to hold the door for women and people coming behind you, and to also be a leader and let your friends or peers know when something is not cool to be doing. I teach them to look people in the eyes when you talk to them and to respect everyone. I teach them to be aware of your surroundings and to leave when you see people doing the wrong things. As I have begun to teach these things to my boys, I realized it is only right to spread those teachings to the black and minority youth as well. A lot of our youth are lacking these skills and these skills are small gestures that can help keep them away from false judgements about blacks and even keep them out of trouble. Like I have mentioned throughout this book, it starts with our mindset, and we must change how we think we should act or ways we must live. We must stop doing things that the world expects us to do and has brainwashed us to believe this is how blacks operate. We must take pride in being black and understand that being black is a positive thing and can be used in a positive way for not only our own culture, but for this country and world that we live in.

We must be on our straight and narrow. We must start using our actions in a positive way. As a culture we need to use our influences and talents in a positive way. The youth today are very creative and have a lot of different resources that we didn't have before. The youth need to use these resources and talents in a positive way instead of falling victim to laziness and excuses. With that being said, it is our responsibility as the older generation to help the youth spark their path to focus on the straight and narrow. We must help the kids that need help with schoolwork and that have trouble with learning. We must continue to let them know how important gaining knowledge is, and that no one can take knowledge away from them. We must help them focus on playing a sport, learning to play an instrument, and showing them things of culture. We must get them off the corners where trouble is inevitable or get them from watching hours of TV where time and opportunities are wasted. We must show them different experiences, such as taking kids on trips to see other cities and countries or taking them to nice restaurants to experience a nice dinner with a nice atmosphere and vibe. When we keep our next generation busy doing positive things and seeing things that are different than our own culture, it keeps them out of trouble and on a straight and narrow path.

The title of this chapter is STAY on the straight and narrow. The key word is STAY, but before you can stay on the straight and narrow, you must get on the straight and narrow. This is for all my youth that have been in trouble, that don't think they deserve certain things, or don't think people will give them another chance. Once again this is all about your mindset and also about the self-love and confidence you should have within yourself. I truly believe people deserve second chances and sometimes third chances. We are all human and make mistakes, especially as youth we make a lot of mistakes. Mistakes are a part of the journey, with that being said with a change of mind-set and some guidance the troubled youth can get on the straight and narrow path. First thing that must happen to get on the straight and narrow is to seriously forgive your-self and let go of the troubles of your past. No matter how you are judged or how someone else portrays you, the only judgment that matters is God's judgment of you and your own judgment of yourself. Once you have forgiven your-self you have to start changing your environment and the people around you. You must look at the things and peo-ple that had you in troubled situations before and start to change that circle. Sometimes you must make tough deci-sions and cut people off when trying to grow and change. When truly trying to change everyone doesn't understand your growth and won't be a part of your new path, but when you turn right onto the straight and narrow those people must be left behind. But to get to this point of being on the straight and narrow after having issues or a trou-bled past starts with YOU. I love seeing a black youth doing positive things. Even more, I love to see a black or minority youth that took it upon themselves and changed their lives around after having issues or a troubled path to start to do positive things.

Blacks and minorities are very important to this country, especially the youth. The youth will become our next law-yers, doctors, teachers, artists, and politicians who will lead into the future. As the world changes for the better when it comes to equality, our black and minority youth must be ready to make the difference. Blacks and minorities must watch the way we move and operate in a world that waits for us to mess up. We must think twice before we make a decision and watch how we handle situations. Instead of always judging each other, the black community must start coming together to support one another. We must lead by example, lend a hand when needed, and share knowledge. One of the keys to helping the youth get on the straight and narrow is explaining to them that the older generation is just like them and to gain their trust. Sometimes there can be a big disconnect between the youth and older generation. It can be the music we listen to, the regions we are from, clothes and shoes we wear, etc. But, as the older generation, we have a responsibility to help the young blacks of the next generation to be better than we are. We must be mature enough to put differences aside for the betterment of the young blacks and minorities, and for the betterment of the world we live in. As the older generation we must respect that it is not about the now, and we may not see the benefits of what we are teaching, but it is our duty to pass the torch of knowledge and encouragement to our black and minority youth. Once we can get past our differences with our youth, we can focus on gaining their trust and letting them know we support them. As they gain our trust, it will be easier for them to embrace what we are teaching to help them get on and stay on the straight and narrow. It is hard to trust older people that criticize and look at them the same way the world does. Instead of passing judgment, we need to let them know we encourage them. Let them know we made mistakes along the way and give them knowledge to help them not to make the same mistakes again. It is so important to show love, to lead by example, and to spread knowledge to the young blacks and minorities. Other cultures seem to cultivate their own kind without any issue, so I challenge older blacks to come together to teach what being on the straight and narrow is and the youth to take pride in taking that straight and narrow path.

Doing the right thing and staying on the right path is called the straight and narrow path because there are always distractions to your left and right that you can turn to, and a narrow path is hard to walk on without falling off. I am the first to tell you IT AIN'T EASY to stay on the straight and narrow. It is so easy to do wrong or to go down the wrong path. I was always told as a kid, "if it is easy to get then it is not worth it and there is a catch." The same concept applies to your life. Doing the right things and going down a positive path may be tough at times, but it is well worth it for your sanity, for your life's opportunities, and for your kids and future generations after you. We must support each other to do the right things and to achieve our goals as well as build up our culture and to change our narrative. We deserve so much as a culture, but doing the wrong things or putting ourselves in the wrong situations pushes us further back from what we deserve. As I continue to say, doing the right things is a mindset, and if we grasp that mindset while focusing on the positive, we will get everything that we deserve and things will continue to change for our culture. Even if it is at a slow but sure pace, it is better than a standstill or reversing pace.

CHAPTER 10:
THE CHANGE

T HE KNOWLEDGE, ADVICE, and experiences in this book will not change the world. They will not stop racism or stop the mistreatment that goes on in this world that we live in. But this book is structured to help change the mindset of the young blacks and minorities. We must change the narrative of how the black and minority life is scripted in America today and how it has been scripted for hundreds of years. The way this country was constructed was made to be against us since our ancestors were forced to come here. Our ancestors were brought here as property and not considered humans. Our ancestors fought hard to get looked at as human and get the rights of everyone else. A lot of the time we take this for granted. We are already pushed behind the eight ball, but the way we handle ourselves as a people and community is making it easier for the "white man" to continue the plan of their ancestors. We must start by making changes and making these changes a priority. It starts with our mindset and we must believe that we deserve better. With that mindset you will love yourself and your people and community. Believing you deserve better is deeper than just you alone; it means we as a people deserve better and that we deserve the blessings that everyone else in our country are able to achieve. That mindset will provide more love for each other where we can help one another achieve our goals as blacks or minorities, stop the violence against each other in our communities, and be like other races and ethnic groups and help build up our people and community. This concept is not hard at all, but it starts with how our mind is programmed. Once that mindset is manifested, like many other cultures, then we can teach our kids how to take routes that will help them prosper. First, we must instill the right values in our youth and how to love themselves, their own people and then all people. We can help grow their knowledge with knowing the law, money management, and reading efficiently. We can teach them the importance of saving and having good credit. Those things are the foundation to start a person's life off in the right direction. It is disturbing to know that other cultures teach their kids the importance of learning and education first while we tell our kids to pick up a basketball or football. As blacks with the talents we have we should be giving our kids a basketball or football and a book at the same time. Letting them know that their brain is just as important and powerful as the God-given talents they have.

The change in mindset doesn't change the struggles of this country but gives us a chance to get a piece of the pie, which we deserve just as much as any other group of people, in my opinion. The changes that we must make will give us a better chance to stay out of jail, give us the knowledge we need to make the best out of our lives, and get out of the system that is built to keep us at bay in every way of life. I look at my boys and see so much potential and so much greatness, but I also feel a fear of what this world and country will do to them if they don't have the knowledge, guidance, or mindset that I am teaching in this book. I feel that same feeling for every young black or minority in this country. I see the greatness and potential in them, and I see things in them that they don't see in themselves yet. But in a lot of them I see the lack of love, lack of guidance, and lack of knowledge that can change their lives. I want the best for the next generation, but every black and minority, young and old, deserves better. I have said a few times in this book that this information is not just for the younger generation of blacks and minorities, but for all blacks and minorities that have been ignorant to certain things that others wanted them to not be knowledgeable about. Some of that is not their fault, some people didn't care to learn, and some didn't think they deserve that aspect of life. Regardless of the reasons, I beg to differ, and I want the best for all blacks and minorities. I want us all to be able to experience the finer things in life, whatever that may be for each person, and also build our portfolio and take on different opportunities that are there for the taking. What would make me happy and fulfilled with this book would be that the information and knowledge that is being spread helps young blacks and minorities earlier in their lives than when I learned these things. I started to really take life seriously and became hip to game on the things I am teaching at the ages between 28-30. It is a blessing that I have never been in trouble with the law, always been organized, always wanted to get degrees, and always had the drive to be a leader and boss. With that being said, no one taught me the importance of having savings, how credit affects my life, what a financial portfolio was, and how not to live paycheck to paycheck. No one taught me how to look a person in the eyes when you are having a conversation no matter if it is an easy conversation or difficult conversation. No one taught me to open doors for women or anyone coming in behind me or to always say "thank you" and "please". By God's grace, these are things I learned on my own by observing other men. I read a lot of different books and learned by looking at men that I admired as husbands and dads, having good careers, achieving their goals, and handled themselves in a way that modeled success. I made a lot of mistakes along the way, but I truly believe my journey is not just for my success and blessings, but most importantly my journey and knowledge are to help not only my sons to be better than me, but to help black and minority youth around the world. The things that I am expressing in this book are just the tip of the iceberg when it comes to saving, investing, building your brand, and changing your mindset. Everyone is different and every journey is different. I would like blacks and minorities to use these things I am expressing as starting points to your development to being greater or add-ons to your development of being great. Life is all about loving and helping each other and I love all people, races and ethnicities, but I am no fool and I see where the ball has been dropped for hundreds of years. And that ball has been dropped when it comes to my people and our culture. It's no secret that blacks and minorities have always been treated less than. The white culture has always had better schools, better resources, and are treated better in society. It is a hurtful truth, but it is a motivation for me to help bring up our culture and help make a change. My way of helping is on a smaller scale, but if I can help one young man or young woman in my culture change their life or gain the knowledge to better their lives then I did my job. As I have said throughout the book, your circumstance shouldn't take over your life. Blacks and minorities may not have the best education system or schools, but we have schools. We may not have the best neighborhoods, but we have homes. It is not fair that things are like this, but instead of using these things as excuses, let's use them as motivations. If there are opportunities or chances, let's take a chance and use the opportunities.

We have to be better and work harder than our white counter parts to get a piece of the pie, but my mindset is if there is a part of the pie to get, I will work to get it. The key word I used is WORK. Blacks and minorities need to embrace the process and embrace the work that needs to be put in to get that piece of the pie. We cannot focus on what other people have or the route they took to get to their success; we need to trust God and focus on our goals and achieving those goals. The foundation of this book and the foundation to achieve better for ourselves has been to change our mindset. As a people a lot of the time I feel we are lazy, content and have a feeling of being entitled. In a lot of ways I feel this is true, but to change that narrative we have to work for what we want. Laziness is a very addictive disease and it can rub off on others around us. But the same way that laziness is addictive, so is motivation and the mindset to be a go getter. Our mindset needs to change from saying things like, "I can do this later", and "I have time", to saying things like, "It is my time", and, "Let's get all we can out of our lives". Because while being lazy is one of the worst actions, being content is not far behind. Being content in the place you are and not having the drive to get better is just an extension of being lazy. And while we are content or lazy as a people, other cultures and races are being go getters. They are supporting each other, setting goals, achieving goals, and making things happen. While blacks are a part of the accomplishments of other cultures because their accomplishments affect the world and society, blacks are not leading these accomplishments and changes. I want my people to lead these accomplishments and changes. Not to just be a part of them, but be the main part of them. All I want is to see young blacks and minorities doing well in many parts of their lives. I want us all to broaden our horizons and get a taste of success. Not just for ourselves but to begin to build generational wealth instead of generational poverty. I want our culture to understand we do deserve better and there are avenues to get that better that we deserve. I want our culture to build each other up and lend a hand to each other instead of hating on each other and killing each other. I want our culture to continue to break barriers and change the narratives that have been a part of our country and world for hundreds of years. These things are not something that will change overnight, but they are things that can happen with a change in mindset and consistent growth in our actions. We are an important part of this country and world, and when we understand that as a unit the changes will continue to happen and the opportunities are endless. Blacks and minorities deserve better, there is no question about that. But blacks and minorities have to want better and to believe they deserve better. I hope this book opens some eyes for someone and helps lead them to bigger and better things in their lives. I hope the information and knowledge I am sharing leads to changes in our culture and helps us as a people to get our piece of the pie. Young blacks and minorities, you are our future and you matter. No matter where you come from, what mistakes you have made, or what someone has said about you. You are important and we have to start loving each other, supporting each other, and helping build each other up. Because WE DEFINITELY DESERVE BETTER!

ABOUT THE AUTHOR

NEVER IN A million years did I think I would have written a book, let alone a book inspired by so many experiences and knowledge gained to help encourage others. Never in a million years did I think I would have been so encouraged by this book that I would have more ideas to create other books to come. The reason I say this is because I was a young black kid born in Norfolk, VA and moved to Atlanta, GA when I was 4. I was raised in Atlanta and I am Atlanta to the core. Growing up, my parents worked hard to make sure my brothers and I were in a good position to succeed, but along the way I have seen things that could hinder that success.

I've seen drugs in my community, gangs, tension with law enforcement and every other hurdle that could keep me behind the eight ball and make me another statistic. What kept me from falling into these worldly traps were sports, school, and opportunities. I was a hooper and I loved school. When I was around 11, I went to Spain with a program called People to People. You had to be a student athlete to be accepted, and what the program offered was for young children to be able to play their sport abroad. I was fortunate enough to be able to go to Spain for a summer to play basketball, where not only did my team win our tournament, but I also won MVP of the tournament. This experience showed me that there is more in the world than just Atlanta, GA. This experience also was the start to my love for traveling. When I began my journey in college, I had my first son as a sophomore and decided that in order to provide, I had to make a drastic decision.

So, I went into the military and did 4 years in the U.S. Army. With this opportunity, I got to travel more and finish my education, which are two things I loved. God has blessed me in my journey and I have gained a lot of knowledge throughout the years. There are a lot of young people from where I am from or places like it around the world that don't or haven't had the opportunities that I have been blessed with, but that doesn't mean they can't get everything they deserve out of life. That is what inspired this book. I am a God-fearing man, a husband, a father, a Veteran, a sports fanatic, and a person that wants to help others.